Lost Souls

Samuel G. Mobley

WESTBOW
PRESS®
A DIVISION OF THOMAS NELSON
& ZONDERVAN

This book is a work of non-fiction. Unless otherwise noted, the author and the publisher
make no explicit guarantees as to the accuracy of the information contained in this book
and in some cases, names of people and places have been altered to protect their privacy.
WestBow Press books may be ordered through booksellers or by contacting:

WestBow Press
A Division of Thomas Nelson & Zondervan
1663 Liberty Drive
Bloomington, IN 47403
www.westbowpress.com
1 (866) 928-1240

Scripture taken from the King James Version of the Bible.

ISBN: 978-1-9736-6637-0 (sc)
ISBN: 978-1-9736-6638-7 (hc)
ISBN: 978-1-9736-6636-3 (e)

Library of Congress Control Number: 2019909018

Print information available on the last page.

WestBow Press rev. date: 07/23/2019

Dedication

This book is dedicated to lost souls, wherever they may be at this point and time in their lives. The main goal of this book is to reach out to them and hopefully lead them to lives filled with hope. Jesus told us to go and present the gospel to a lost and dying world. With this book, I am trying to achieve that goal. It is not enough for me that I have a personal relationship with Him. I want everyone to share in the joy of knowing Jesus Christ as Lord and Savior of their lost souls.

Jesus is the answer to the problems this world and the people in it face each and every day. Life is not what people think it is. It's not about just you and me. It's really all about Jesus and the reason He came. He came to seek and to save lost souls so that none should perish. The joys of heaven await us all if we just place our lost souls in His hands.

Although this book is dedicated to lost souls, let it also be an encouragement to you who are already Christians. Hopefully, by reading this book, you will be encouraged to go and be a witness for Christ.

Remember, we have the message lost souls need to hear. They need to hear the message we need to share for they may not know, just how much Jesus really cares!

Foreword

What a privilege it is to write the foreword to Samuel G. Mobley's latest book. It is obvious this book was written from the heart of a God-inspired man. I have known him and been his pastor for nearly thirty years. Deep in his heart, he has longed to be of use to God. Through the written word of this book, God has given him that opportunity. Writings like "The Old Book" are sure to touch the hearts of those who read its words. It tells of the wisdom and knowledge of God's Holy Word and will fill your mind with joy and peace. I am sure those who read "God Is Watching Us" will also come face-to-face with the reality that even though we have come so far in our many technological advances, we have as a society actually regressed. It also reminds us that God is watching us to see what we will do!

Perhaps the message in "Do You Sometimes Wish?" will truly speak to your heart. It asks, "Do you sometimes wish for a better place where problems vanish, where hurt and sorrow are no longer there, where disease has fled and tears are no longer shed?"

It is my prayer that the message in this book will draw you closer than you have ever been in your relationship with Jesus Christ. *Lost Souls* is the title of this book, but it is also the target of this book. To reach lost souls with the message of God's forgiveness, by His grace, is the purpose for writing this book.

Sit back and relax as you wander down the road of anticipation, or maybe, the road of memory as you read the pages of *Lost Souls*.

John R. Porter
Pastor, First Church of the Nazarene
Chester, South Carolina

Contents

Lost Souls

I came here to tell a story
That I promise you
Gives me no joy or glory.
This is a story that must be told,
Even though it will not be pleasing to your ear
Nor something you hold dear.

It's the story of lost souls,
The ones left behind,
The ones who chose—
For one reason or another—
Not to believe.
The ones who could not conceive
Of the gift of God.

That One so faithful and true,
So loving, yet so tough,
So tender, yet so rough,
Would die so that we might live.

Lost souls live with regret,
Mostly of the Savior they never meet.
They lost the chance of a lifetime,
Living life from moment to moment,
Never realizing
Jesus came for their atonement.

Lost souls are lost forever,
Never to see what could have been.
All because they chose
Not to follow Him.

Now they will go where lost souls must
Because in Jesus they failed to trust.
They must live with the choices they've made,
And a heavy price indeed must be paid.

What a truly sad and pitiful day
When lost souls go to Jesus
Only to be turned away.
The words they will hear Him say,
"Depart from me; I never knew you,"
Will ring in their ears
For years and years and years.

A Walk on the Dark Side

I took a walk on the dark side.
Man, was that a mistake.
The price I've had to pay
Was not worth the thrill I had each day.

Sure, I had my pleasure.
I looked at what I did as treasure.
I cherished each moment
As if it was my last.
I forgot Jesus
And the price He paid for my atonement.

Each day was filled with excitement.
Doing something almost illegal
And getting away with it
Was a challenge I adored,
An addiction I could not resist.
But it has led to all this.

I am a useless man for God.
My indiscretions have cost me dearly.
In fact, they nearly
Cost me my life.

A walk on the dark side
Has brought me nothing
But pain and misery.
I've lost my wife and friends,
My job, and my kids.

I followed a path that's a mile wide,
And I've paid a heavy price
For taking a walk on the dark side.

Me and God

Do you want to know
What lie has been said,
What thing has been done?
Don't look here nor there
For you will not find
The answer to the question.
Only me and God really know.

Would you like me to tell
Of the things from my past,
Tell of the days
That never really had a chance?
For God was far from my thoughts,
So far away from my heart.

But let me tell you of His grace
And how far I've come.
How, if not for His mercy,
Of death I would soon taste.
Of how, if not for Him,
My life would be a total waste.

Don't dwell on what was;
Rather, on what will be
For my past is not reality.
The here and now is what I am.
Where it all leads
And where I go,
Only me and God really know.

The Wage of My Sin

The crown of thorns they laid upon His head
Should have been mine.
The scars that He now bears
Belong to me.
He felt the pain and agony,
The clothes I should have worn.
He carried to the cross the scorn
And paid the wage of my sin.

The nails, the hammer, the tree,
All were meant for me.
But He, the Savior, took my place.
He showed mercy and grace.

Now I stand on solid ground
Because the Savior, I have found.
He took the wage of my sin
And allowed me to place it all on Him.

Give Me the Words

All alone she stands in the dark.
I should have known things weren't right.
I watched her stare out the window.
I watched her stand there
From morning until night.

Her broken heart lay open before me,
But there was nothing I could do.
Her wounds were open wide,
So I just held her
And stood close to her side.

The words of comfort,
The words of care,
No matter how hard I tried,
The words just were not there.

I couldn't understand why she hurt so bad.
Didn't understand why at God she was so mad.
So I chose to look the other way
For I could not find
The words I needed to say.

Somehow let her draw from You, oh Lord.
Let her seek Your warm embrace.
Let her find sweet peace in Your touch.
Let her find Your loving grace.

So I give You her,
The love of my life.
All I ask from You,
Is stay close to her side.
Don't let her suffer alone in the dark.
Give me the words to say

To heal her wounded heart.

Stumble and Fall

Yes, you'll see me stumble.
And yes, you might even see me fall.
But all of the time I am lying there,
I'm thinking of how I can walk again,
Knowing I must first
Learn how to crawl.

I will soon get up.
Yet I know struggles each day will come.
But I will not be denied
For I know the Savior's will must be done.

It's not for me to say
Why this calamity came my way.
All I know is
I will walk again.
I know I must.
For in Jesus alone do I trust.

His will, will be accomplished in me.
His will must be done.
I promise you, I will see
The day of His return.

For I know one day, Jesus,
I know my eyes will see,
Will come in His own glory
For people who sometimes stumble and fall.
Yes, for people just like me.

The Mask

When you take off the mask
Each one of us wears,
You might ask,
"What will we find
Lurking in the deep recesses of our minds?"

Look in the mirror.
Tell me, what do you see?
A kind, gentle heart,
Or someone just waiting to rip you apart?

So it is with each of us.
That's why in God
I choose to trust.
My faith in Him
Is all that I need.
My trust in His Word
I shall always heed.

His mask is transparent.
He lets us see right through.
He's not like me and you.
He has nothing to hide,
Nothing to lose,
Nothing to gain.
He doesn't hide behind the mask
Of sin and shame.

So whatever you are,
Put your trust in Him
For He knows your deepest secrets.
Yes, He knows each one of them.
It's not that hard a task
For Him to see
What you try so carefully
To hide behind the mask.

The Mourning Dove

We were not expecting what we saw
For the day before was rather uneventful to us all.
But we were left in total awe,
When the mourning dove came to call.

We were telling old stories
About the one we love,
Reminiscing of the good times now gone by.
We knew time was slipping away.
We knew Jesus would soon come.
It might be tomorrow but maybe today.

We would often look out the window
To see blackbirds sitting in wait.
We were taken aback the next morning,
When they failed to show.
Why, we didn't know.

But in their stead was a sign
We were surprised to see.
There all alone sat a bird
We had not yet seen.

It was a mourning dove,
Come to sit and wait,
Come to reassure
As the time was getting late.

The Spirit had come,
Come to be with the one we love.
Come to comfort her
And put our hearts and minds at ease,
Letting us know beyond a shadow of a doubt
Jesus had come for the one we love
In the form of the mourning dove.

The Old Book

I took the old book
And read from its well-worn pages.
Yes, the old book,
Which has stood the test of time,
Stood for all the ages.

I read all the old stories
Told of so long ago.
I marveled as I read each one
And wondered why
Their meaning I did not know.

Reaching for the answers
To questions my life had brought me to,
I continued on my journey
Since I knew not what to do.

Of wisdom and of knowledge,
The old book had so much.
It filled my mind with joy and peace,
And felt warm and tender to my touch.

My eyes beheld its beauty.
With each page that I would turn,
The answer to all my questions lay before me,
As I was soon to learn.

I laid the old book down
On my nightstand.
I drifted off to sleep,
Knowing Jesus would hold my hand.

Through the night,
Through the storm,
Or whatever comes my way,
I learned from the old book
He is with me,
Come whatever may.

The Promised Land

Even though dark clouds hovered over me,
Yet I was set free from the chains of sin and death.
No longer do I hide in the shadows.
I am now a child of the light.
No dark clouds,
Nothing but blue sky,
And Jesus is the reason why.

He reached way down
To pull me out of the darkness.
His light shone bright around me.
He saw me in my distress,
And He answered my call.
He held me in His hands
And welcomed me to the Promised Land.

A land flowing with milk and honey,
Where a tear never falls,
Where death never calls,
Where peaceful waters flow,
And the fruits of the tree of life grow.

A land where time is no more
And where life never ends.
Where disease has fled,
And tears are no longer shed.
Where joy and laughter fill the air,
Where sorrow and sadness are no longer there.

Yes, this is the Promised Land.
Heaven is now my home.
It's here where I now stand.
It's here where I belong.

Headstones

I took a walk through the yard.
Went to visit Grandmaw, Granddaddy, Mom, and Dad.
I have to admit
After a short visit,
I was a little sad.

I looked around and saw all the headstones.
I was left in total awe.
So many lie before me.
Some up close, some afar.

I wondered who they belonged to
And what had been their demise.
I looked at the one beside me,
And much to my surprise,
A headstone with a message
That brought tears to my eyes.

These simple words were all it said:
"I've been forgiven.
How about you?
Jesus died for me
And also for you."

So simple a phrase.
So strong a meaning.
Those words of wisdom
Rang loud and true.
I knew right then and there what I must do.

So I fell to my knees,
Whispered gentle and true,
"Father forgive me
For I know not what I do."

Answers to Questions

I went to the park
Just to sit and think.
Before I knew it, it was dark.
Time had passed by
Quick as a wink.

I suddenly realized
I was all alone.
I looked around and noticed
Everyone had gone.

Lost in my own thoughts,
I had lost track of time.
I kept wondering how
I had gotten from here to there.
Kept wondering what had led me to the here and now.

Questions started running through my mind,
Like, where do I go from here?
What's my next step?
Will anyone help?
What if I am totally on my own?
What lies ahead?
Will it even matter after all is done and said?

Even more questions flooded my mind,
Like, which way do I go?
Will I succeed?
Will I fail?
Does it really matter?
Am I just chasing my tail?
So many questions,
So few answers.

Answers to questions are like,
Looking for the light at the end of a tunnel.
You know it's there,
But you just can't find it
For the darkness surrounds you.

It's like looking for a needle in a haystack,
But the stack is so high,
And the task so great.
Or trying to find the end of a string
In a ball of yarn.
You know it's there,
But where?

So many questions
And many to ask.
So few answers
And few who know them!

Curtain Call

This is it!
Never had I been so nervous.
Never had I been so apprehensive.
This night, however, was different than most others.
All of my family was there—
My mother, my sisters, and my brothers.

This would be my final performance,
My last curtain call.
I was hoping not to mess it up
For it had only been a short while
Since I had my tragic fall.

I had become a shell of my former self.
I had lost everything, including my wealth.
But most important, I had lost my health.
It had even become a chore
Just to get out of bed
And walk out the front door.

Life handed me up on a silver platter,
Picked me up and spun me around.
When people asked, "What's the matter?"
I just looked at them with a frown,
Turned my back,
And without saying a word, walked away.
I would even eventually leave town.

I had grown extremely tired
And oh, so very weary.
For no matter how hard I tried,
Life just seemed so dreary.
There was no way out.
It made me want to just scream and shout!

But then I met a man
I'd never seen before.
He stood outside my house
And knocked on my front door.
I asked Him in.
He said, "Why sure.
I've come here just for you.
I've come to make all things new.

Now let Me carry the load.
That's far too much for you to bear.
For I've made a place in heaven
For you and others like you to share.

Now it's time for you to enjoy
Your final curtain call.
Go and face the music.
You'll see it's not so hard after all.

Everyone will be so proud of you.
You just wait and see
For everyone will stand
And give applause
For the life you led for Me!"

Early Morning Walk

Hello, God.
I've been missing our talks.
But today,
When I went for one of my early morning walks,
I noticed something quite odd.
You were still there,
Like we had not been not talking at all.
I knew You were there
For Your presence filled the air.

I know You were wondering why I was so silent.
It wasn't that I meant to be.
It's just so many things are bothering me.
I need the ear You so often lent
When we used to have those special talks
During my early morning walks
Through the garden.

From the dust of the earth You made me.
You breathed the breath of life into me.
I was not, but then I was.
You placed me in Your garden
To work and watch over it.
But that was not enough;
I wanted more.

You said it was not right for me to be alone,
So You made living creatures
And let me name them one by one.
Whatever I called them,
That's what they were.
But they were not like me.
Human company is what I need.

So when I went to sleep,
You took a part of me.
You gave me what I wanted,
When all I really needed was You.
The one you gave was bone of my bone,
Flesh of my flesh.
Woman, my helpmate,
Together we became as one.

You gave me all,
And yet I had a terrible fall.
The temptation from the tree
Was far too great for me.
Our talks have now become infrequent
All because of me being delinquent
In my relationship with You.

But You made another way.
You sent your Son, Jesus Christ, to save the day.
He died on a tree
So that You, oh God, and me
Can have a little talk
When I go for my early morning walk.

God's Watching Us

If God looked down from heaven,
Like He always does,
Say it's a quarter past seven,
Is everything as it was
a few years ago?

If it is,
Do you think God is pleased?
Before you put your mind at ease,
Remember, God's watching us,
And in Him we are supposed to put our trust.

You know God lets us do
What we want to.
He gave us a free will,
But it doesn't give us the right to maim and kill.
We just can't do any old thing
And expect God's blessing
For we are not a king
With no one to answer to.
You see, God's watching us.

Society thinks we've come so far
When, in reality, we've actually regressed.
So many of us are still repressed
All because we chose our own way.
The results are heartache and dismay.

Instead of putting our faith in God,
We choose to follow the path of man,
Even though
We know
It's not in God's divine plan.
Remember, God's watching us.

There was a time when we depended on God.
Now we depend on ourselves.
Doesn't that seem quite odd?
We had no doctors, lawyers, or politicians.
God was the Great Physician.
God wrote the laws.
He alone was the ruler of the universe.
We danced to the beat of His drum.
Now to the beat of man.
Isn't that quite dumb?
People, God's watching us!

You know, it's never too late
To turn things back around.
God wants to hear us pray
When we see our erring ways.
God's watching us to see what we will do
For in our hearts
We all know His words are true.
Now what do you think we should do?
Remember, God's watching us.

I Did It Very Well

God gave me the challenge.
I took it based on faith.
He told me, "I will be with you."
I told Him, "You must
For in You alone do I trust."

But my time is at hand,
And my days are now few.
I've said all I can say.
I've done all I can do.

So I say these words
Straight off the cuff,
Hoping You'll say,
"Well done, my child.
Enter in, you've done enough."

This is it!
Lord, I'm done!
I've laid it all on the line.
I gave it all that I had.
There's nothing left to give.
I have tried my very best.
Now it's time for me to sit and rest.

I've said all that needed to be said
And said it very well.
I did all that was required and more
Before I turned out the lights
And walked out the door.

Was it enough?
Only time will tell.
But I did the very best that I could,
And I know in my heart,
I did it very well.

I Was Just Thinking

I was just thinking the other day
About how things used to be.
About how much things have changed,
Of how far we've come,
Of how close we are to oblivion.

The plan was to live in peace,
Make the world a better place,
Do away with the normal day to day,
Get out of the human rat race,
Create paradise here on earth.
But hate and greed only made things worse!

Even now, wars and rumors of wars
Never seem to cease.
In fact, we've only made a crease
In our efforts to live in peace.

I thought time and education would be the answer,
But we are still in the same boat.
If we continue on this course,
Our problems will only get worse.

And modern technology,
What did that do?
Computers were supposed to ease our workload,
But all it did was create job overload.

A one-world economy might have been the answer.
But all it did was make things worse than ever.
I was just thinking,
Has anything really gotten any better?

In His Hands

Christ holds my life in His hands.
In spite of what life demands—
What I am,
What I become—
All depends on Him
For I can do nothing on my own.

I must follow the path He has chosen for me.
I could not, not do
What His divine plan has in store
For I am lost in this world of endlessness.

To become someone great
Or someone small,
No matter which,
It's all for the glory of God
For He alone is in control.

My successes or failures
Lie solely in His hands.
For no matter how hard I try,
I could never do it on my own.
I must follow the path He chose for me
A long, long time ago.

To deny it now
Would seem somehow
To deny Him,
For who He was,
For who He is,
My Savior,
My hope,
My guide.
My life truly is
In His hands.

Live and Die Free

On foreign soil, the soldier dreams
Of his homeland far away.
For it doesn't always seem
It's worth the price he has to pay.

You know, life is not always pretty
When the battle lines have been drawn.
For the soldier must stand and fight
From dusk until dawn.

He wonders if people really understand
What a soldier goes through each day.
For with each day comes
Death, heartache, and dismay.

Still, the soldier chooses to fight one more time,
Knowing all along this day could be his last.
But a soldier stands tall
And is up to the task.

So off to the battlefield he must go.
For he made the choice long ago
To stand and fight for the country he loves
And for the ones he holds near and dear,
So we all do not have to live in fear.

On this Fourth of July,
Let us give thanks
To the God on whom we rely
And then to the soldiers
Who give their lives to God and country
So that you and I
Can live and die

Free!

My Little Trip

I have been on a trip.
Took me a little vacation.
I had decided to slip
Away for a while,
Take a few steps back,
Reassess things,
Get my life back on track.

I happened upon an old man
Traveling down the road.
I decided I would stop and help.
At least see if I can
Maybe lighten the old man's load.

I gave him a lift to the next town.
Turns out he lived just down the street.
Said he preached at the local church,
Where all the good folks like to meet.
Asked me if I would visit,
I said sure, I would
If I could.
But I had no desire to.

Sunday morning came,
And what do you know,
Nothing but rain
And the wind with a heavy blow.
I decided to take the preacher up on his offer,
So off to church I went,
Even though I thought my time
Could have been better spent.

I got there just in time for preaching to start.
There he was, all shined up, looking the part.
He talked about Jesus
And what He had done.
How He had come
Just to save lost ones.
How He came,
Even though
He would pay a price with His life.

Despite it all,
He did what He must
Just to make a way for all of us
So that we can be with Him
If only in Him we put our trust.

That old, gray-haired preacher said,
"Repent, and give your heart to Christ."
He gave an invitation.
He did not have to ask me twice.
I went right then to the altar,
And gave my heart to Christ.

Wow, what a nice little trip.
Never thought I would say,
"What a beautiful day
With no sunshine, pouring rain,
And a day of vacation spent in church."

God sure changed my little trip.
I took a journey everyone must take
If they want to reach heaven
Before it's too late.

Relax

Have you ever wondered
Why things seem to never
Turn out the way you want, ever?
You would think after a lot of planning,
Things would come out just as you thought.
But sometimes things just don't work out as they ought!

We can't always make it come true
Just because we want it to.
Sometimes the law of averages catches up to us,
And everything falls through our hands, like dust.

Learn to take things in stride.
For from your problems
There's just nowhere to hide.
You can't always push the limits.
If you do,
Sooner or later, something is going to break,
And it just might be you.

Learn to lean on Jesus
For He will see you through.
He will always be with us
Through the good and the bad times too.

As you go through this life racing,
Take time to relax from the battles you are facing.
Sit back and relax.
Let everything go
For Jesus will be there to lighten your load.

He is the Master of the wind and waves.
He alone is the One who saves.
So when life has got you taxed,
Give it all to Jesus,
And just sit back and relax.

Robe and Crown

Standing right before your eyes is a miracle.
You see, I was the scum of the earth.
But now I've experienced a spiritual rebirth.

I was a man filled with hate,
A man torn between death and life,
A man worn from the trials of life,
A man lost in a world of sin,
A man who had no way out
For my mind was filled with self-doubt.

I could not see
For the veil of sin covered me.
Now I rise from the ashes of that sin,
Purified by the blood of Jesus,
Filled with the Holy Ghost,
Led by the almighty hand of God.

Now, no power can hold me down.
Nothing can keep me from the love of God
For through His grace and mercy,
Jesus made a way for me
To one day wear a robe and crown.

The Words You Say

Is what you say
Really what you mean?
Or are they all just words,
Hollow with no meaning?

I hear what you say,
But are you saying what I hear?
Please make it abundantly clear
So I want take the wrong way
The words you say.

I need to know what you really mean,
Or the words you say won't mean a thing.
They will be like a banging drum
Or a clanging cymbal,
Just a whole lot of noise
Without nothing really in them.

I would rather hear the words of dread
Than to listen to you speak
Without nothing ever really being said!

The World as One

I will write of your glory
And tell the story
Of the man who died for me.

I will sing a new song
When men and women give their hearts
And start
To praise You all day long.

When the world finally sees
And turns from its wicked ways,
We will see
How it truly can be.

It will be a world without end,
Filled with joy and happiness.
A world where laughter fills the air,
And pain and sorrow are no longer there.

A world where we can find peace,
Where once lost souls can find rest
Under the wings
And in the nest of
Jesus!

With God as our leader
And His Son at His side
And the Holy Spirit as our guide,
The world will be as one.
It will become
The true paradise it was meant to be
For you and for me
For all eternity.

Seasons

Summer, winter, spring, and fall.
The seasons of the year
Appear once a year,
Each with its own blessing or curse.

Some like it hot as in summer.
Some cold as in winter.
Some like spring,
When new life bursts forth,
Others fall,
When the leaves turn,
Giving the landscape its rich colors
Of ambers and yellows.

Life is a lot like the seasons.
Spring, being a newborn,
Everything around you
Is brand new.
Each new day throws you a fastball or curve.
But that's how we learn,
So when we grow older we don't crash and burn.

The long, hot summer,
Man, what a bummer.
This is the time in life
When things really heat up,
The lightning and thunder part of life,
When we go through a lot of heartache and strife.
But it's all just part of living life.

Then fall comes around.
The air gets a little cooler.
The grass starts to fade.
The leaves begin to turn
And then gently fall to the ground.
It's the time of life
When retirement enters our thoughts.
Or did we get done
What we thought we ought?

And finally, winter arrives
With its cold blustery mornings.
It's a season of trying to keep warm
And hoping the pipes don't burst.
A time in life we don't often cherish
Because we know
It's not long before we perish.

Where did time go?
How did winter get here so fast?
We all knew this would not last,
So here we are.
What do we do
Now that our seasons have past
And our lives are now through?

So Strangely Familiar

Being here is so strangely familiar.
I know I've been here before, but I haven't.
Everything seems so real, yet unreal.

Maybe I dreamed all of this.
Did I have a vision?
Did God sweep me away
To let me know
I would see all of this one day?

The walls are of jasper,
The gates of one single pearl.
My, what a beautiful world.
I know I've never been here,
But it all seems so strangely familiar.

This place is so bright,
And I've noticed there is never a night.
And talk about clean.
Man, those city streets just gleam!

Everyone walks around with a smile;
I never see a frown.
Time doesn't even seem to matter;
I haven't seen a clock,
And no one wears a watch!

All of this seems so strangely familiar,
Even though
I know
I've never been here before.
Yet none of this seems peculiar.

This is the place generations have longed to find.
A place I've only been able to picture in my mind.
I've finally seen paradise.
God has allowed me to see it
With my own two eyes,
And it all seems so strangely familiar.
Isn't that quite peculiar?

Things

I've accumulated a lot of things over the years,
But none as important as seeing someone come to Christ.
Oh, I'm grateful for the things,
But I've come to realize, at this point in life,
There is so much more.
More than my eyes can see,
More than words can say,
So much more than the day to day.

I thank God for
The roof over my head,
The shoes on my feet,
The clothes on my back,
For food on my table,
And a great job that allows me to do
The things I want to.

You know God has things too,
Like grace that falls like rain,
Healing to ease my pain,
Salvation that can save a soul,
Comfort when darkness surrounds
And I've grown tired and old.

God has given me all of the things I need.
Now let me give to Him the thing He wants most—

Me!

Time to Reap

A piece of land was bought.
A very select piece I would say.
Bought with the blood and guts
Of the man who died for me,
The Man of Calvary.

The soil was tilled.
The seeds were planted.
Fertilizer was applied.
The field was showered with rain
And bathed in the warm sunshine.

We watched the seed grow
And weeded the field with love.
We threw out the rocks
So their growth would not be slowed.
The work was done,
And the seed had its time to bloom.

Now the field is ripe for harvest.
The reaper has come.
No more time is left;
His will must be done.
It's time to reap
What has been sowed.
Ready or not,
Here He comes!

To Live

The day was sunny and bright,
A warm summer's delight.
Not a cloud passing by,
Nothing but blue sky.

It had rained during the night,
Watering the grass and flowers.
I sat on the front porch swing,
Just watching them grow
As if nothing really mattered.

The air had a fresh scent,
And the flowers were in full bloom.
Didn't know what it all meant.
Didn't realize the impending doom.

A messenger came and went.
Devasted, he fought to find the words.
He told me of what he had heard.
A dear friend had passed away.
He died alone, all by himself.
It had happened just yesterday.

I reminisced of our past
And wondered,
What made us think life would never end?
We knew in the back of our minds
Nothing ever lasts.
But you know how we are.
We tend to cling to the past.

I chose to forget what I had heard,
Even though it left me quite disturbed.
After all, it wasn't me.
I still have a lot of time left;
I still have things to do.

I have no time to give,
Only life to live.
I chose to forget
The next time it just might be me
Who steps out into eternity.

Too Late

While the whole world
Runs around in turmoil,
We sit quietly, patiently
Waiting for the Savior's return.

It's not that we aren't scared.
It's not that we don't care.
We are not immune to danger
Or the hazards of life.
It's just that we don't worry
Or get in a hurry
When the things of life
Cause heartache and strife.

We choose to have faith
In the Father, Son, and the Holy Ghost.
We believe in the three in one.
And when all of life is done,
That is what will count the most.

The hustle and bustle of life
May get you there fast,
But it will not last.

When time is no more,
And we're standing on heaven's peaceful shore,
To have gained the whole world
Would not compensate
For having died,
Lost in our sins,
Knowing it was too late.

Trying to Find My Way Home

You know, sometimes you go down a road
Thinking it's the right turn,
But maybe you should have turned left.

Right now, I feel like
I'm on the outside looking in.
Like I'm walking through the darkness,
Searching for the light,
Trying to find my way home.

I've been living on the edge,
Way out in the wilderness.
The places I've been,
The things I've seen,
Some of the stuff I've done
Would amaze a normal person.

I've faced many battles.
I've even won some.
A lot of people think it's a big thing,
But I just did what had to be done.
No big deal,
But it was real.

Those battles were something I could feel,
Something I could taste.
It was like breathing fresh air
On a cool fall night.
Everything just felt right!
You know what I mean
'Cause you've been there.

But lately, I've had a change of heart.
Maybe I should have taken a different path,
Taken that right at the fork in the road
Instead of a left.

I've recently spent some time just thinking
About this living and dying thing.
You know, it's got me asking questions.
What happens when life ends?
Does it all end with death,
Or is it just the beginning?

Is it a time for joy
Or a time for sorrow?
What if I die tomorrow?
What would it have all meant
If I haven't spent
My life serving Christ?
For we all know He gave it all for us.

I'm on the outside looking in,
Walking through the darkness,
Searching for the light,
Trying to find my way home.

We Should All Just Quit

There's more to life
Than sittin' back and soaking it all in.
This just can't be it!
If it is, we should all just quit.

God has not called us to sit and wait.
He's called us to take charge
Before it's too late.
We can't be just lying around, waiting.
We must be anticipating
The move of the Spirit!

We must get out of our seat
And get on our feet.
For there's a lost world
For us to meet.

We must continue on,
Even if we are battle weary and battle worn,
We must not give up the fight
Until we see heaven's glorious lights.

Remember,
We have the message
They need to hear.
They need to hear
The message we need to share
For they may not know
Just how much Jesus really cares.

May I?

All of these things keep coming at me,
Hounding me, until I cannot rest.
Now it's up to You, oh Lord,
For You know I have done my best.

Will You show me the path?
Will You lead me beside the still waters?
May I be far from Your wrath
And counted as one of your sons and daughters?

May Your grace shine down on me.
May Your hand be upon me.
May Your touch heal my wounded soul.
May I behold
The awesome power of Almighty God!

Dear Lord,
May I be called a Son
Even though I am unworthy?
May someone like me
Be counted in the number?

Will you remember me
When my life is at hand
And my days are past,
So I can at last
Be with You?
May I?

Someone Just Like Me

When my days were dark and drear,
I often wondered if He could hear,
Hear the desperate plea
Of some poor lost soul,
Someone just like me.

Even when I had to face the toughest test,
I always hoped for the best.
I have always hoped He would be there
To guide the footsteps of a man
Willing to follow Him to who knows where.
Maybe someone just like me.

I have tried very hard to prove my worth,
But so often I was overlooked.
I tried so hard to let them see
That God could use
Someone just like me.

I always knew He would be there,
There, to watch over me,
To guide me safely through,
To let me know He cared
For someone just like me.

Even though I could not see or feel His presence,
I knew I was never far from His grace.
My only hope was disgrace
Would never come from someone just like me.

I know my life has sometimes let Him down.
Lots of times I should have been wearing a smile
Instead of a frown.
But He understands the difficulties I face
For often He has forgiven me
And washed away my transgressions,
Leaving not a hint or trace.

I don't understand why God chose me
For I am just a man of humility.
But for some strange, unexplainable reason,
God always chooses to use
Someone just like me!

Stop and Listen

Stop and listen.
Be amazed at what you hear
For the sounds of His returning
Are oh, so very near.

Listen to the seven angels
As they blow their trumpets loud.
Listen to them blow them
Strong and proud.

They're sounding the alarm
For those lost in their sins,
Sounding it for those
Who were lost, but are now born again.

The end is coming,
With its plagues and death.
Nothing can stop it,
Not even the world's power and wealth.

Nothing can stand up
To the power of an Almighty God
For He is the One
Who controls this earthly sod.

So people, please be ready
For He's coming with His staff and rod
To cleanse and redeem this world
From the turmoil and sin that it adores.
For these are the things that our Lord and Savior
Totally abhors!

Stop and listen.
Listen while you can.
For someday very soon,
Disaster will strike this land.

Listen to the sound of His voice
Before the last trumpets blow.
For if you do not give your heart to Christ,
Off to hell
You will surely go!

Stand Alone

Here I am, just sitting here,
Staring at these walls.
It seems as if no one cares
Because there is no one to share my misery.
So I just sit here wondering,
How do I fight the battles alone?

My friends have all left,
Gone to seek fortune and fame.
Gone to the world of man,
Gone so far away.
I can only hope one day
They will find their way back home.

They chose to leave
When things got tough.
It's so hard for me to believe
That they would leave
When the going got rough.
But they turned and ran away.

We had made a vow
All of us swore not to break.
I just don't know how they could;
It's just so hard for me to take.
But I must go on
For there is still a war
That must be won.

Despite what they did,
I shall not give up the fight.
Even though I have to fight the battles alone,
I shall stand with the enemy, toe to toe,
And match him blow for blow.
For I know
God shall be with me.

In times of weakness,
He will make me strong.
From dusk until dawn,
He will give me the strength I need
To defeat my enemies
And shine His guiding light
Through the storm and through the night.

Though I must climb high hills,
Walk through valleys dark and deep,
Scale mountains rugged and steep,
Even face the enemy face-to-face,
I know God will always be with me.

Even when everyone else turns tail and runs,
I shall stand,
Even if I have to stand alone!

The Lord Would Be There

I was lost in the darkness,
Somewhere lost in time.
I couldn't find my way.
I had no peace of mind.

I looked here and there.
I looked everywhere,
But I found no peace within
For I was lost in the darkness.
I was hiding deep within my sin.

I looked high and low
But had nothing to show
For all that I had done.
I was all alone,
With nowhere to go.
It looked as if again,
Satan had won.

I had my doubts
Of ever finding my way out
Of the mess my life had become.
But something deep inside
Told me to go
Where we all know
The answers I would soon find.

So I opened up the book
In which I was so often told to look,
Hoping to find my way,
Hoping to find
The Lord would be there.

But I had never really seen,
Nor did I know what it would mean
If I chose to follow Him.
Follow Him to who knows where,
Even if I knew wherever I would go
The Lord would be there,
Listening to my every prayer.

So I decided to take a chance on God,
Even though some might think that rather odd.
But I had tried the ways of man,
Tried to do things my own way,
Which brought me nothing
But heartache and dismay.

So here I am, Lord, I'm Yours.
Now help me find Your way
For I need Your heavenly touch
To guide me each and every day.

Show me the love You gave
In the forgiveness from Your Son.
For I need the love You've always shown—
The love I have always needed,
The love I have never really known.

If I should ever stumble,
If I should ever fall,
I know the Lord will be there
To listen when I call.

Help me have the faith,
When trials and troubles arise,
To do whatever it takes
When the world trembles
And the earth shakes.

Let me be faithful and true
No matter what men say or do.
For if trouble should ever come my way,
I now know the Lord will be there
To meet the need of my every care.

Looking and Hoping

I wondered what had happened,
What had led to my demise.
So I looked in the mirror.
I searched deep within my eyes.

I opened up my mind.
I took a long, hard look,
But I could not find the reason
For my treason,
Or why I had fallen away.

I had paid a recent visit
To my darker side,
And now the price I must pay
Just cannot be denied.

I kept looking for a way to hide my sin.
Kept hoping time would make me forget.
But it only got worse
The longer on it went.

So I tried to forget
That I had gone astray.
But the thought of what I had done
Kept getting in the way.

I tried with all of my might,
And even though I am quite strong,
Nothing I had found
Could cleanse me from my wrongs.

So I started looking
In God's Holy Word,
Hoping I would find out
That it was true,
The things I had heard.

I was hoping Jesus would forgive and forget,
Maybe looking for Him to turn the other cheek.
For I knew the Man who had done no wrong
Held forgiveness in His hands
For those who in a moment had gotten weak.

So I read John 3:16
And Romans 6:23.
I read about the wages of my sin
And how Jesus had died to set men free.

I skipped on over to Ephesians 2:8 and 9,
And there I found what I had been looking and hoping for.
God's grace was full and free.
If only I would ask,
It would be mine.

So I took the gift He offered—
Forgiveness from my sin—
Hoping that I would never do
What I did ever again.

But I know He'll forgive me
If I should ever fail.
For His grace is all sufficient,
And He knows I yearn to do His will.

Lord, I Tried

I understand the grief you bear,
But there is nothing you can do.
I, too, lost my mother.
I suffered just like you.

I could have given up,
Turned and walked away,
But she would not want that.
That's why I'm still singing today.

You see,
God called me,
Not just her,
And now that she is gone,
Things can never be as they were.

I must face the battle.
I cannot give up.
I cannot give in.
For if I do,
Satan wins again.

Though it's hard,
The battle for lost souls goes on.
God's call on our lives must not be denied
Until we breathe our last breath
And utter to Him,
"Lord, I tried."

Inside of Me

Everyone thinks I'm okay.
They think I'm doing fine.
But they don't see the misery
That's going on inside of me.

I'm left with the scars,
Shattered by the words,
Haunted by the memory
Of things from my past.
But each day I put on my smiley face
And reluctantly join the rest of the human race.

I dress to impress.
I shine my shoes and comb my hair.
I even take a look in the mirror
When no one is there,
Always hoping no one will see
What's really going on inside of me.

I cover my pain
With a joke and a hearty laugh.
But if everybody really knew
I'm about to fall apart,
They might look at me with disdain,
Turn their heads and walk away.

So I'll hide behind this wall I've built—
So sturdy, stout, and tall—
So no one will see
What's really going on
Inside of me.

I Don't Want To

(The Christian's Statement)

I don't want to
Live my life looking back over my shoulder.
I don't want to
Live my life wishing I would have done more
Before I got older.

I don't want to
Live my life waiting for something to happen
For I know sometimes in this life,
You've got to make it happen.
For time waits for no one,
And there are things in this life that must get done.

For a long time, I carried the world on my shoulders,
Trying so hard to get it right.
Nothing was too tough for me.
I did it all,
And I did it diligently.

But life has a way of wearing you down,
Tearing you apart,
Chewing you up,
And spitting you out.
Leaving you left for dead,
Lying on the ground,
Alone and cold.

But somehow,
Like a phoenix rising from the ashes,
I got up to face another day.
Though I got knocked down repeatedly,
Spat upon, and thrown to the lions,
I just kept getting back up.
I never, ever quit!

I guess it all comes down to this:
You just can't keep a truly born-again Christian down!
Even when we are wearing a frown,
We are still smiling inside.
For we have the blessed assurance
Of the Holy Spirit being our Comforter and guide.

You might call me a glutton for punishment,
But I refuse to let this world keep me down
For I have this:
Jesus died for my atonement!

I don't want to,
And will not by the grace of God,
Allow a man or woman or anything to
Stop me from achieving my goals,
Even when I have grown tired and gotten old.

I don't want to
Hear people tell me I can't do it!
Or it can't be done,
Or it's impossible.
For the battles I face each day must be won.

I have found
If it's God's will
And I do it God's way,
I will be successful,
Regardless of what "they" say.
Or I will die trying.

When my life is a closed door,
I don't want to
Look back, wishing I had done more.

Only One

There is only One
Who can touch the sun.
Only One
Who can kiss the moon
And hold the stars in His hands.

There is only One
Who can mend a broken heart.
Only One
Who can save a dying soul.
Only One
Who can guide me through the night
When the fire has gone out,
And I'm alone and cold.

There is only One
In whom I can trust,
Only One.
To worship Him I must.
Only One
Who died in my place
In the darkness of sin.
Yes, only One
Who has walked
Where none of us have ever been.

There is only One
Who can calm a raging sea.
Only One
Who can set a man free.
Only One
Who can make a lame man walk.
Only One
Who can loosen a tongue to talk.

There is only One
Who could have hung on a cross.
Only One
Who could have died for the lost.
Only One
Who can save a person from sin.
There is only One:

Jesus Christ!

God Can

God can turn nothing into something.
Make less become more.
Turn a dream into reality.
Take hope and make it real.

God can turn doubt into belief
With faith from above.
Make an honest man out of a thief,
And do it with His abounding love.

God can move mighty mountains
And calm the raging seas.
Take the strongest man alive
And bring him to his knees.

God can take the vilest sinner,
Wash his sin-soaked stains away.
Turn a loser into a winner,
Make him see the better way.

God can turn someone you hate
Into someone you can love.
Mend a broken heart
With healing from above.

God can do a lot of things
If we will just get out of His way.
Even turn your darkest moment
Into your brightest day.

Man thinks,
I can do it without God,
But he always seems to fail.
For he always thinks he's got the answer,
When he's really only chasing his tail.

God Has a Plan

I was totally on my own;
No one was there.
The burden I had to bear
Lay on my shoulders alone.

There were no instructions to follow,
No etched in stone plans.
Not even a diagram to go by.
It was placed in my hands.

But I knew deep in my heart
God has a plan,
And God's plans never fail
For He alone is in control
Of my life and of my soul.

You know God has a plan
That includes each and every one of us.
If we will only take it out of our hands,
And in Him alone put our trust.

If we will one day say,
"I accept His perfect plan,"
He will then once again
Be the ruler of our land.

While on this earthly sphere we roam,
We will then no longer be on our own.
For God will be with us
To guide us,
To lead us,
To help us find the way.

If we would just realize God has a plan
And not try to do it on our own,
He will etch it on our hearts
And burn it deep within our souls.
The plan that is oh, so simple,
And oh, so very well known.

"For God so loved the world
That He gave His only begotten Son
That whosoever believeth on Him
Shall not perish,
But have everlasting life"
(John 3:16).

Do You Sometimes Wish?

Do you find yourself
Just going through the motions?
Do you sometimes wish
You could do whatever you want,
Whenever you took a notion?

That no matter what comes your way
You can just brush it aside,
Or find a nice, quiet place
Where you can just go and hide?

Do you sometimes wish
You could just fly away,
Way out into the clear blue sky?
Maybe lie down on a nice, soft, fluffy cloud,
And let the world below
Rush on by?

Do you sometimes wish
You could go on to heaven
And leave your cares behind?
Where there is no pain and sorrow,
And no one cares about tomorrow?
Where everyone is gentle and kind?

Do you sometimes wish
You could just run away,
Find a nice, peaceful place,
A place where dreams become reality,
And the trials of life vanish without a trace?

Do you sometimes wish
You could go somewhere
Where problems vanish into thin air?
Where hurt and sorrow are no longer there?
Where disease has fled,
And tears are no longer shed?

Do you sometimes wish
The world would just go away?
Do you sometimes wish?

Almost Ready

You are almost ready,
But not yet quite.
Time for you
To see the light.

It's time for you
To think about the end.
Time to think about
What will happen then.

You are almost ready
To walk through those pearly gates.
Almost ready,
So don't wait until it's too late.

Get your act together
For the time is oh, so near.
For it won't be long
Before Jesus Christ shall reappear.

He's coming back
For those He has claimed.
Coming back
For those who believed in His holy name.

He's almost ready
To break the eastern sky.
He's almost ready,
So tell this world goodbye.

Take the advice of the Master's plan
For almost ready will not get you in.
Listen to His voice while you still can.
For there will be no more chances
For those lost in their sin!

He's Coming

Don't put your trust in the one
Who brings impending doom.
Rather, put your trust in whom
The wind and the waves obey their commands.

For He's coming with His mighty swift sword.
He's coming, our Savior and our Lord,
Coming to bring joy and happiness.
Coming to bring healing, hope, and peace from distress.

He's coming to reap the harvest
That has been sowed.
Coming to get
His chosen ones.

He's coming, quick as a flash.
In a moment no one knows.
He's coming with His army of angels
As long ago in the Bible it was foretold.

He's waited forever;
Or so at least it seems.
But He's here right now,
Fulfilling the Christians' dreams.

As the story of old fully unfolds,
The dead in Christ shall rise.
And those on earth quickly changed
Right before your very eyes.

As the beast and his armies
Run away in defeat,
They will soon be kneeling at Jesus's feet,
Proclaiming He is who He said He was,
The King of Kings,
The Lords of Lords!

Challenges Ahead

Thanks for all you've done for me.
It's given me the courage to leave.
I would not know what to do
If it had not been for all of you.

There are challenges ahead for me
That I must now face,
Even though it would suit me just fine
To just let them be.

But I have to run this spiritual race
For my heart yearns to serve God
And to experience His powerful, merciful grace
And His awesome, wondrous love.

You see, I have been called of God
To travel this foreign land,
To seek the ones who are lost
And those not yet found,
And place them in His loving hands.

Called to win those who have turned away
Only to be left for dead.
Called to win those
Who have fallen from grace
And now of their lives
They totally dread.

This journey will lead me down many paths.
Some filled with heartache, and some with pain.
And I know I will feel the devil's wrath
While helping others find peace and hope again.

Some challenges will come with joy and laughter.
Some challenges with sadness and tears.
I will have some wins and some losses
As I continually serve God over the years.

So now it's time to go.
Where this journey takes me
I really don't know.
But I will remember the times we shared.
I will remember just how much you cared.

I will think about what is yet to come,
Think about His will to be done,
But never forget my friends back home
No matter how far I go
Or where on this earth I roam.

Now I must move on
For there are challenges ahead.
And I must face them one by one
For I know the Lord is soon to come.

Pray for me as I walk this path.
Pray that I will be all I can be
So that others may see
Jesus Christ, my Lord and Savior,
Living in and using me!

In His Own Time

Jesus will return in His own time,
And even though
Many have tried to predict
The calamities of all of it,
The day of His returning will be
In His own time.

Even though
They don't know the season,
They try so hard
To find the reason
Why these things must come.

And they search for a sign
That they will never find,
Often making themselves look
Rather dumb.

In His own time
He will come for His chosen ones.
But He will not come for all.
For the unsaved will regret
The Savior they never met
When He often came to call.

People wonder when He will come
And why He has waited so long.
All not knowing
The day of His returning,
For them He was slowing,
So His grace,
On them it would fall.

What He does on that final day
Will amaze us one and all.
As He streaks across the eastern sky
To the sound of the last trump,
The redeemed will hasten to His call.

Now let us be ready.
Stay firm and steady.
Don't let your fire go out.
For the day of His return
Might come quicker than you think.
In the twinkling of an eye,
Quick as a wink.

All I Ever I Wanted

All I ever wanted
Is held in God's hands.
All I ever wanted
He gives without demands.
For He loves me like none other,
Even more than a father or mother.

God has supplied all of my needs,
Even things of silver and of gold,
Most of which eventually turned to dust
Or fade away with time and then to rust.

The things that matter most
He gives an endless supply.
But when He gave me
Forgiveness, hope, and love,
He gave me all I ever wanted,
And He did it, without batting an eye.

All I ever wanted was to love
And be loved in return.
He gave me that and more,
Even though the gift He gave
I, for so long, chose foolishly to ignore.

All I ever wanted
Was to live in peace
With my fellow man,
Then die and go to heaven
As God laid out
In His divine plan.

When He let His own Son
Die on the cross for my sin,
He did it
So that I would not be lost.
So that I could be free once again.

He showed me His unfailing love
By doing what He did.
And when He gave me forgiveness,
He gave me
All I ever wanted!

Absolutely Nothing

Let me tell you, people,
This one fact,
And I probably won't do it
Using very much tact.

There is absolutely nothing without God,
Nothing to see or hear.
Nothing to smell, taste, or touch.
He created it all
Because He loved us so much.

Now, to those who will listen
With open ears,
Let me tell you what I know,
Tell you what I have learned
Over all of these years.

When all is said and done,
And all of life's battles fought and won,
I would have absolutely nothing
If not for the grace
To run the race
I have run.

I would have absolutely nothing
If I could not trust in God's Holy Word.
Absolutely nothing
If the message of salvation
I had never heard.

Absolutely nothing
Had He not saved me from my sins.
For where would I be then
If I didn't have Him?

I would have absolutely nothing,
Even though I may have all things of this world.
For the things of this life are worthless,
Even diamonds and pearls.

Even if I had all the riches of this world
But did not have Christ in my life,
I would be one miserable human being.
For without Christ,
I would have absolutely nothing.

No car anyone has ever owned,
Nothing anyone has ever done,
No house anyone has ever built
Would mean anything
If not for the blood,
Of Jesus Christ being spilt.

Life would be totally meaningless
Without the forgiveness
That comes from Almighty God.
And to live it, absolutely ridiculous
Without the grace that He affords.

When my days are gone,
When my final, last breath has been drawn,
I will leave this old world behind
And take with me to heaven

Absolutely nothing!

A Wise Man

A wise man will serve God
And Him alone.
A wise man will leave his own desires
And follow the path of Christ
For he knows his work is all in vain.
What he achieves on earth is worthless
For death awaits us all.

A foolish man's treasure lies in the grave.
There, wasting away
With his old, dry bones,
His worldly treasures turn to dust
And blow away with the wind.
He never realizes
The true treasures in life
Come from God!

A wise man learns from his past mistakes
And those who have gone before him,
While the fool repeats history.
He never learns from "the Teacher."

A fool walks his own desperate path
Filled with heartache and destruction,
Always thinking he knows the way,
When all along,
The path he was on
Could never have been more wrong.

Such is life, as we well know.
Shall we choose the old path well worn,
The one that leaves us
Empty and torn?

Shouldn't we learn from our past,
Move on to something that will last?
Shall we not choose the path of life
Like a wise man would do?
Or shall we play the part of a fool
Like we so often choose to?

So would you rather be a wise man
Or play the part of a fool?
Would you rather be a wise man
Or be the devil's tool?

The Rapture

Where did they go?
They were here just a minute ago.
Now they are long gone,
Like they never existed.
Vanished into thin air
As if they were never there.

In a moment,
In the blink of an eye,
They were no more.

I could not understand
What was going on.
A few here and a few there,
This type of thing
Was happening everywhere.

I can vaguely remember
Of a story told of old,
How people lost and now saved
Off to heaven they would go.

They called it the rapture,
Or being caught up in the sky.
Although I am not sure,
They said it would happen
When a man named Jesus came by.

They would take nothing with them—
Not their silver, nor their gold—
For their treasure awaits them in heaven.
Or so, as I remember, the story was told.

I guess the story slipped our minds.
I guess we all forgot.
But I wish I had remembered
For it caught me by surprise.

Now of this story's reality,
I am completely sure.
For I heard it and I saw it
With my own two ears and eyes.

Nothing could compare
To what happened on that day.
It happened in just an instant.
It happened just as the story did say.

The sad thing is
I'm left here with sadness and misery.
Left here with the pain and agony
Of knowing I was left behind,
Of knowing what awaits me.

The things the story told
I must now endure.
All because I forgot the warnings
Of the story told so long ago,
"The Rapture."

The Storm

As the storm began to form,
I watched with blinded eyes,
Seeking to hide with disguise
While Mother Nature gave her warning signs.

We thought we were safe
From its ominous look.
We thought we were free from fear.
So casually the storm we took.

A mighty rushing wind
Began to blow with a howl
As the storm clouds grew
And the rains fell.

The clouds grew to a darkened black.
And the rain fell with a rushing pour
As the flashing lightning clashed,
And the thunder blared
With a terrible loud roar.

I saw it coming with my own two eyes.
Quickly it came,
And then it passed.
I saw it come and then go.
How I survived it,
I still don't know!

And when it was all over,
When all was said and done,
There was nothing left
But total devastation.

The storm had left its path of pain and misery,
Leaving us to pick up its scattered debris.
Nothing like this had ever happened before.
And I pray to God
It doesn't ever happen anymore.

The Man of God

I thought I saw the Man of God,
Standing right over there.
I thought I heard His voice,
Telling me to make the choice
To follow Him to who knows where.

Then He came, and then He went,
Even though I hoped He would stay.
For I wanted to know
Of the price for my sin,
Why would He be willing to pay?

The Man of God
I heard so much about
Chose to save me from my sin.
The Man of God
Who hears a lost soul's prayer
And answers each one of them.

When He came to visit me
On that warm summer day,
He took every one of my sins,
Placed them on His back,
And carried them far away.

A lost soul's prayer was answered
When He showered me with His saving grace,
Leaving me without a trace
Of the sin I had so long embraced.

Now I am a free man.
Free from sin's cold, hard embrace.
For all of my sins are now gone
Thanks to the Man of God,
Without a memory or trace.